My African Rainbow

By
Jada Free

This book is dedicated to every little boy and girl that see's magic in every moment.

Wisdom is wealth. ~ Swahili

A **Rainbow** is an arc of colors that appear in the sky opposite the sun. It is caused by the sun shining through the rain, mist or spray.

My AFRICAN Rainbow has colors
that are just for me. My AFRICAN
Rainbow has colors that only I can
see.

I See Purple so beautiful and
strong.
I See Green magnified with
greatnesses.

My AFRICAN Rainbow has colors that are just for me. My AFRICAN Rainbow has colors that only I can see.

I see **Black** so mature and smart. I see Red so passionate for the future.

My AFRICAN Rainbow has colors that are just for me. My AFRICAN Rainbow has colors that only I can see.

I see Silver so peaceful and pure. I see Gold so mighty and noble.

My AFRICAN Rainbow has colors
that are just for me. My
AFRICAN Rainbow has colors that
only I can see.

I see Blue filled with love and
peace.
I see Yellow so precious and
abundant.

My AFRICAN Rainbow has colors
that are just for me. My AFRICAN
Rainbow has colors that only I can
see.

I see Pink so wise and kind.
I see Maroon so healing and
warm.

My AFRICAN Rainbow has colors
that are just for me. My
AFRICAN Rainbow has colors that
only I can see.

I see Grey so vibrant and new.
I see White so festive and fun.

My AFRICAN Rainbow has colors that are just for me. My AFRICAN Rainbow has colors that only I can see.

What colors did you see?
Did you see the same as me?

Now you give it a try. Let's make an African Rainbow for you too. Remember each color has a meaning.

1. Black – maturity
2. Blue – peace, harmony and love
3. Green –growth, vegetation, planting, harvesting
4. Gold – royalty, wealth
5. Grey – healing and cleansing
6. Maroon – Mother Earth & healing
7. Pink – associated with the female essence of life
8. Purple – associated with feminine aspects of life; usually worn by women
9. Red – political and spiritual moods.
10. Silver – serenity, purity, joy
11. White – purification, sanctification rites and festive occasions
12. Yellow – preciousness, royalty, wealth, fertility

All by yourself...

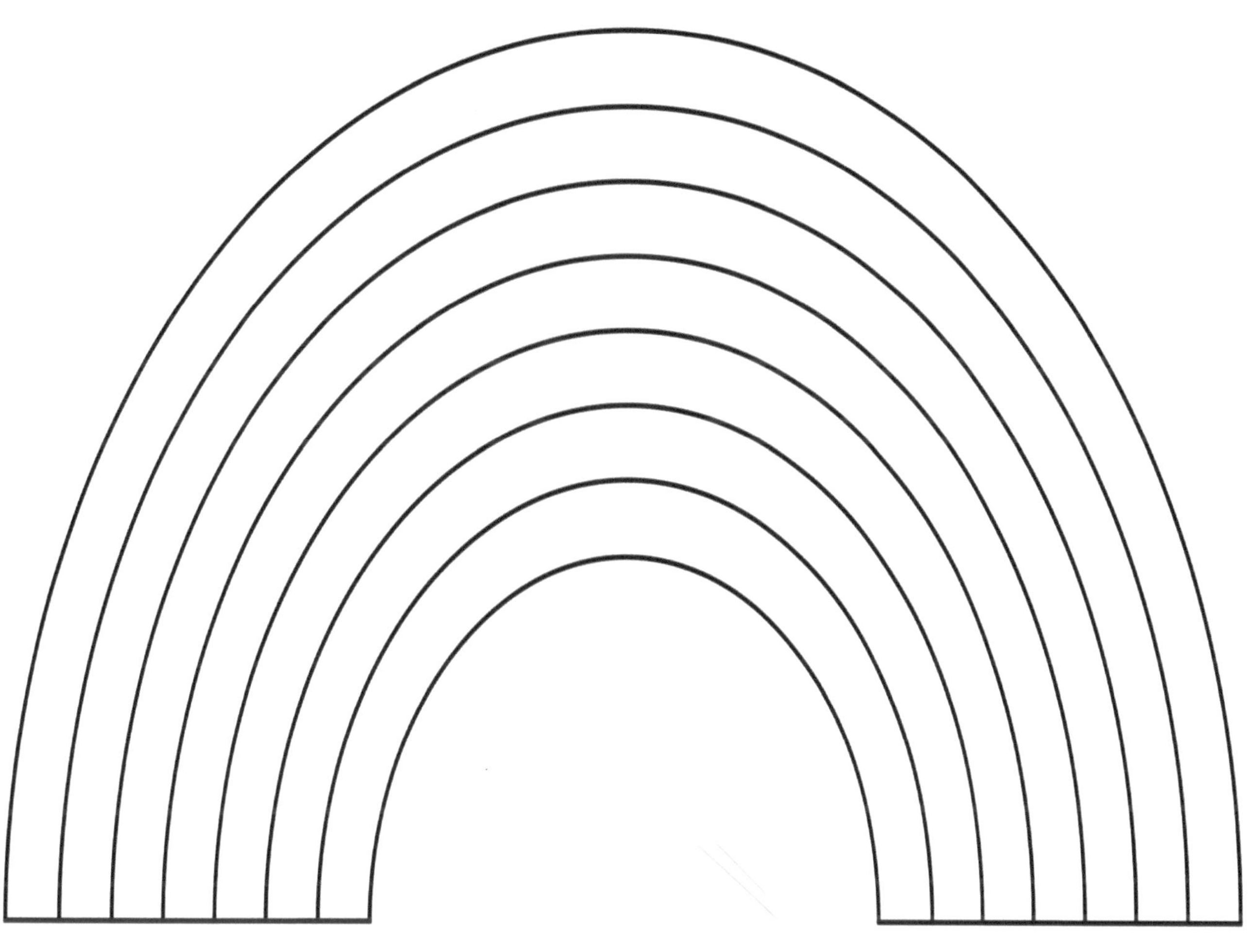

Or with a friend...

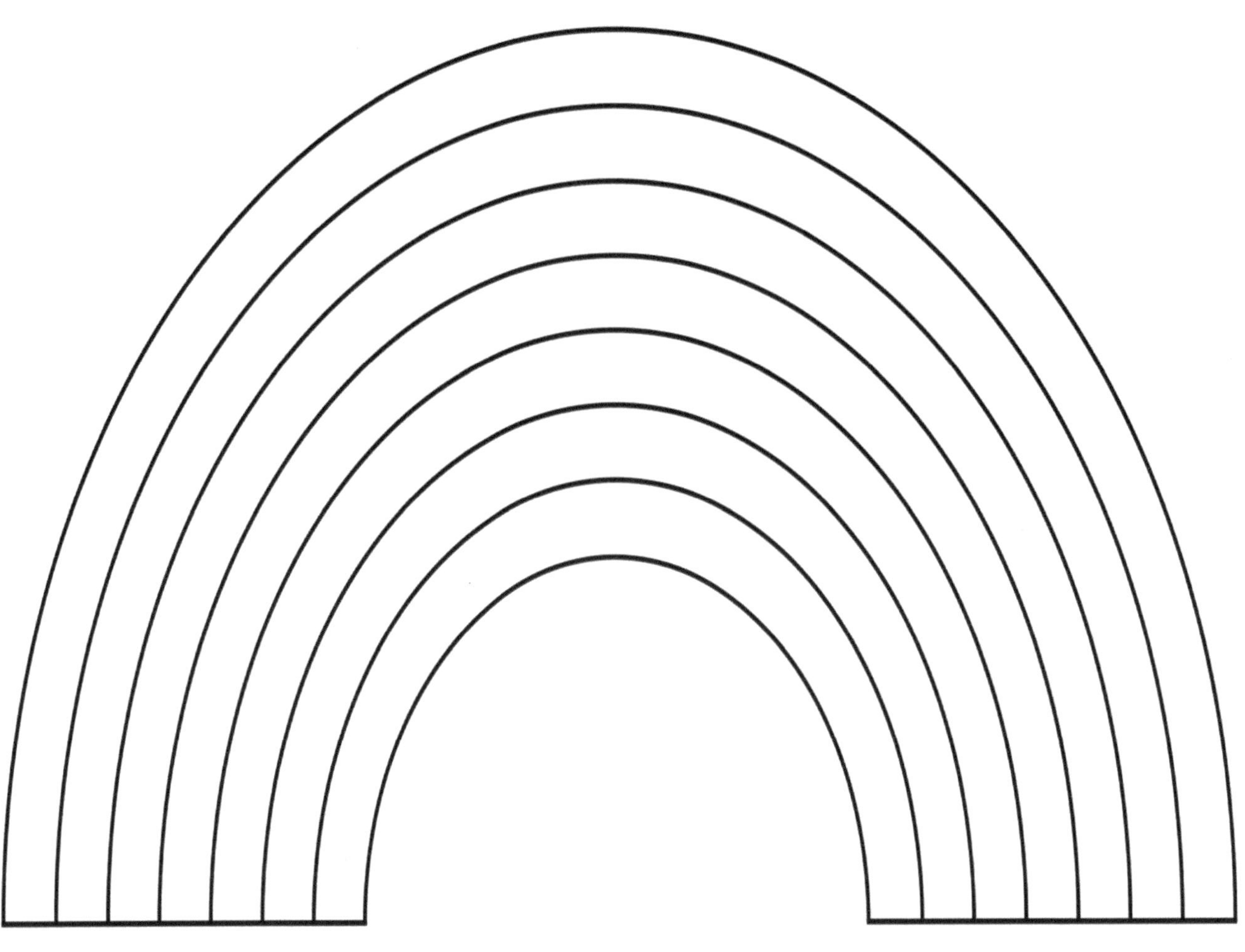